**Also by Julie Dunlop**

*Ocean of Yoga*

*Honoring the Light in You*

*Thousands of Years of Prayers*

# Earth, Water, Fire, Air, Space

## Meditative Poems

*poems by*

# Julie Dunlop

*Finishing Line Press*
Georgetown, Kentucky

# Earth, Water, Fire, Air, Space

## Meditative Poems

Copyright © 2024 by Julie Dunlop
ISBN 979-8-88838-741-2 First Edition
All rights reserved under International and Pan-American Copyright Conventions. No part of this book may be reproduced in any manner whatsoever without written permission from the publisher, except in the case of brief quotations embodied in critical articles and reviews.

Publisher: Leah Huete de Maines
Editor: Christen Kincaid
Cover Art: Julie Dunlop
Author Photo: Karen Dunlop
Cover Design: Elizabeth Maines McCleavy

Order online: www.finishinglinepress.com
also available on amazon.com

Author inquiries and mail orders:
Finishing Line Press
PO Box 1626
Georgetown, Kentucky 40324
USA

# Contents

Dear Reader, .................................................................................... xi

Abundance ........................................................................................ 1
Alchemy ............................................................................................ 2
A Tree of Mirrors .............................................................................. 3
Ancestors .......................................................................................... 4
Anemone ........................................................................................... 5
Archeology of a Moment ................................................................. 6
Archipelago ...................................................................................... 7
Architecture Within ........................................................................ 8
Beyond .............................................................................................. 9
*Bīja* ................................................................................................. 10
Birdsong .......................................................................................... 11
Blessing ........................................................................................... 12
Bloodwork ...................................................................................... 13
Bone Blessed .................................................................................. 14
Brocade ........................................................................................... 15
Butterfly .......................................................................................... 16
Cartography ................................................................................... 17
Center-Song ................................................................................... 18
*Chelonioidea* ................................................................................. 19
Cicada Song ................................................................................... 20
Circling ........................................................................................... 21
Cocoon ............................................................................................ 22
Collaboration ................................................................................. 23
Colors Reconfiguring .................................................................... 24
Cores Steady .................................................................................. 25
Could You Become ........................................................................ 26
Courage .......................................................................................... 27
Cradling Dissonance ..................................................................... 28
Crosspollinating ............................................................................ 29
Dawn ............................................................................................... 30
Deciphering .................................................................................... 31
Dimensions .................................................................................... 32
Early Morning ................................................................................ 33
Earth Day ....................................................................................... 34
Earth's Aria .................................................................................... 35
Elixir ............................................................................................... 36

Encircling..................................................................................................37
Excavation ................................................................................................38
Facets.........................................................................................................39
Fire Song...................................................................................................40
Forgetting .................................................................................................41
Formlessness and Form ........................................................................42
Galaxy Within.........................................................................................44
Geography................................................................................................45
Geology of Breath..................................................................................46
Gone Now.................................................................................................47
Grasslands ...............................................................................................48
Harvest......................................................................................................49
Heard and Unheard...............................................................................50
Heart Song................................................................................................51
Heat ...........................................................................................................52
Herald .......................................................................................................53
Hope..........................................................................................................54
Impermanence........................................................................................55
In the Silence in Between ....................................................................56
Inside the Flow.......................................................................................57
In the Mind .............................................................................................58
Interwoven ..............................................................................................59
Into Equilibrium....................................................................................60
Jewels........................................................................................................61
Koan..........................................................................................................62
Letting Go................................................................................................63
Liminal.....................................................................................................65
Listening to the Underside of Leaves...............................................66
Looking Within .....................................................................................67
Looking: The Five Elements...............................................................68
Luminous.................................................................................................71
Lung Song................................................................................................72
Mist............................................................................................................73
Monsoon..................................................................................................74
Murmurations........................................................................................75
Night's Choir ..........................................................................................76
Ocean of Peace.......................................................................................77
Of Breath and Bone...............................................................................78
Offertory..................................................................................................79
Of Silence and Rain..............................................................................80
One Syllable............................................................................................81
Orange......................................................................................................82
Our Tongues Split.................................................................................83
Owl............................................................................................................84

| | |
|---|---|
| Pangaea | 85 |
| Pattern | 86 |
| Perching Inside the Soul | 87 |
| Portal | 88 |
| Prairie | 89 |
| Prayer Circles | 90 |
| Quilted | 91 |
| Radius | 92 |
| Remembering | 93 |
| Resilience | 94 |
| Resonance | 95 |
| Rippling | 96 |
| Rivers | 97 |
| Ruins | 98 |
| *Scherzando* | 99 |
| Singing Bowl of the Heart | 100 |
| Sitar's Song | 101 |
| Small Spaces | 102 |
| Smoldering | 103 |
| Sometimes It Is the Not Saying | 104 |
| Song of the Potomac | 105 |
| Temple Inside | 107 |
| The Current, the River, and the Rain | 108 |
| Through a Deepening Mist | 109 |
| Transformation | 110 |
| Transliterating the Silence | 112 |
| Tree of Tranquility | 113 |
| Unencumbered | 114 |
| Universal | 115 |
| Unseen | 117 |
| Unspoken | 118 |
| Untouched by Sour Sirens | 119 |
| Vanishing Point | 120 |
| Vestiges | 121 |
| Voice | 122 |
| Wild Mint | 123 |
| Winter Solstice | 124 |
| When All Else Fails | 125 |
| | |
| The Journey of This Book | 127 |
| Gratitude | 128 |

# Acknowledgments

"A Tree of Mirrors" originally published as "On Route 4, Returning from Jemez Springs" in *New Mexico Poetry Review* (2012)

"Bloodwork" published in *The Journal of the American Medical Association* (JAMA) 317 (14):1483: April 11, 2017. Copyright 2017. American Medical Association. Reproduced with permission. All rights reserved.

"Facets," "Formlessness and Form," "Geology of Breath," "Interwoven," "Letting Go," "Looking: The Five Elements," "Of Breath and Bone," and "Portal" published in *Breath, Bone, Earth, Sky* (Finishing Line Press, 2014)

"Grasslands" published in *South Dakota Review* (2003)

"Excavation" published in *Baltimore Review* (2005)

"Lung Song" published in *The Journal of the American Medical Association* (JAMA) 305 (5):443: Feb. 2, 2011. Copyright 2011. American Medical Association. Reproduced with permission. All rights reserved.

"Mist" published in *Bending Back the Night* (Finishing Line Press, 2012) and originally published in *Appalachian Heritage* (2005).

"Ocean of Peace" published in *Ocean of Yoga* (Singing Dragon, 2017)

"One Syllable" published in *The Journal of the American Medical Association* (JAMA) 321 (19):1940: May 21, 2019. Copyright 2019. American Medical Association. Reproduced with permission. All rights reserved.

"Ruins" published in *Eureka Literary Review* (2005)

"The Current, the River, and the Rain" published in *Breath, Bone, Earth, Sky* (Finishing Line Press, 2014) and originally published in *Janus Head* (2011)

"When All Else Fails" awarded $1000 Dorothy Rosenberg Memorial Fund Poetry Prize (2006)

Dear Reader,

While we may have never met, we share something in common: the five elements.

In the midst of so much division in society today, we run the risk of losing sight of our shared humanity. We can forget that regardless of profession, religion, age, culture, political party, economic class, or any other factor, we are united in the universal nature of the five elements of our being.

The concept of five elements is central in multiple ancient traditions. For instance, traditional East Indian culture honors the five elements of earth, water, fire, air, and space. These five elements are called *pañca mahā bhūta* in the Vedic wellbeing system of *Āyurveda*.

In simplest terms, we can think of the earth quality of our bones, the water component of the plasma in our body, the fire aspect of our metabolism, the air quality in our breath, and the element of space existing in between the cells of our body.

Remembering the five elements of earth, water, fire, air, and space brings us into a closer relationship with nature. When we stare at electronic devices too long, we can forget the sound of the rivers and oceans, the gentleness of a warm breeze touching the skin, the beauty of the dynamic colors of sunrise, the sweet scent of fresh flowers, the invigorating taste of newly fallen snow. We can forget our divine connection with Mother Nature and lose sight of the fact that by caring for the world around us, we simultaneously support our wellbeing.

The presence of the five elements within us and around us is profound; paying attention to this presence can deepen our understanding of ourselves and how we relate to the natural world, and can ultimately bring a deeper sense of harmony and beauty in our lives.

*Earth, Water, Fire, Air, Space* explores the five elements within us (mind-body-spirit) and all around us, as well as the subtle spaces where the internal terrain and external terrain intermingle. Bringing light to the resonance between the individual and the universal, the poems in this collection celebrate our shared humanity. The poems might become part of a yoga class, a meditation class, or a mindfulness workshop, or enjoyed in individual exploration and contemplation.

May your journey bring you peace.

With gratitude for the earth, water, fire, air, and space all around us and within us,
    Julie

*Dedicated to the elements
of earth, water, fire, air, and space
around us and within us*

~

*Dedicated in loving memory with deep gratitude
to my beloved teacher, mentor, and friend
Dr. Edwin G. Wilson (February 1, 1923—March 13, 2024)
of Wake Forest University, North Carolina
Poetry Professor, Provost Emeritus, Author, and Humanitarian*

~

*Dedicated in loving memory with deep gratitude
to my dear lifelong friend and mentor
Howard E. Cummins (September 22, 1926—September 5, 2024)
of the Appalachian Mountains of Virginia
Author, Columnist, Teacher, Advocate for Appalachian Arts,
Master Storyteller, and Triple-Generation Family Friend*

**Abundance**

Entire communities
  of trees
  meditating[1]

waterfalls
  spilling into
    lakes
  into
      oceans,

moon blooming
  from crescent
    to full,

the air
  pollen-rich,

wildflowers filling
  the hillsides,

fireflies lighting up
  the night sky
  like stars

---

[1]trees meditating: a concept learned from Dr. Vasant Lad

**Alchemy**

Deep within
   the muscles
  of the heart,
past traumas
    sing
   untranslatable songs—
their singular
  sounds
ricocheting off
  walls
turning
  into sunrise,

  the metallic clashes
of long ago
   absorbed
  in an alchemy
of windchimes
   and singing bowls,

the heart
  like a canyon,
    a constellation,
  an ocean

  forgiving,
remembering,
  and letting go—

then shining again,
  with devotion
uncollapsible
  as rock,
sunlight,
  the tide.

**A Tree of Mirrors**

Beyond the small waterfall
where ancient prayers still speak,

beyond the fresh bread at the open market
backdropped by towering red rocks,

beyond the roasting chiles
spicing the air with their sweet fire,

beyond the empty altars
in the sleeping tin-roofed churches,

beyond the oil paintings
humming softly inside adobe walls,

beyond the cornstalks, gourds,
orchards, and fields of alfalfa,

a tree of mirrors breathes light
from an outside wall of a house

nondescript except for the way
its mosaic of swirling limbs

snaps back the sun, dazzling
the dry desert air, the baked dirt,

making of itself a shrine
to light, to all that reflects,

to the beauty that can manifest
when myths of bad luck

shatter one jagged piece at a time—

**Ancestors**

The ancestors lean in,
   listening, gathering
small pearls of sound
   into crescent-moon-
shaped ears
   made of quarks
and particles of light,

   the ancestors moving
quicker than lightning,
   traversing entire countries
in a heartbeat

Embedded in their memory
   like strands of gossamer
the imagery of feet
   walking across the fields,
husks opening
   into perfect ears
of Silver Queen,

the cornstalks swaying
   in a salt-air breeze,
the cries of the gulls
   by the coast
too far away yet
   to hear

**Anemone**

Flowering plants
  of the buttercup family
growing wild
    in fields,
their petals
    of white, purple, pink
      forming
small mandalas
    emanating
from their sacred center,
   sun-sung

Beneath the sea,
   their namesakes—
sea anemones:
   bright pink, orange,
white, green,
    sometimes fluorescent,
pulse:
    their tentacles
moving in the waves
   like petals
fluttering
  gently
  in a
soft
  breeze

## Archaeology of a Moment

Eight guitars.  A picnic table.  No one in sight.
In the distance, a locomotive,
its cacophony of movement churning.
In a graveyard nearby, femurs rattle.
An unceremonial skillet of homemade gravy
sizzles in a bed-and-breakfast over the ridge.
Biscuits, hot from the oven, wait on the table.
Buried signatures of deeds to the land fade.
In the damp coolness of a morning hinting at rain,
the raging wound of a regret softens.
The mythical creature of dream delivers
the tropics, papaya juice sweet like nectar,
weeping willow branches swaying in a breeze,
the song of elk high in the mountains,
a family of walruses, their ivory tusks a-gleam.
Entangling images unquilt themselves
into their singular selves.  The strings
separate from the guitars, the wheels
come off the train, the dreamer waking up
into a dream of a dream, the coveted peace
of a silent symphony hovering just barely
out of reach.

**Archipelago**

In the family
of islands
of thoughts

in the ocean
of the mind,

excavations
ongoing—

relics
of years past
unearthed,
dusted off,

their molecules
breathing fresh air
again,

the lungs
of the past
coughing,
sputtering,

awaiting
   the slow
  deep
elongated
   exhales
of peace

**Architecture Within**

The regal interplay
  of the vertebrae,
the exquisite swivel
  of the hips,

simplicity of symmetry
  in the smoothness
    of scapula's song,

tiny metacarpals
  and metatarsals
enlivening the hands
  and feet,

the shimmering orderliness
  of cuspids and bicuspids,
ineffable elegance
  in the rotation of the wrists,
the flutter of the eyelashes,

  the intuitive way
    the liver, spleen,
and pancreas commune,
  the wisdom of their design,

  and there, at the center
of the forehead,
    unseen,
  a small rose window:
beautiful colors
  of light
    shining through—

**Beyond**

Rosemary, frankincense,
 sage, copal, and camphor,

resplendent flame,
 sweetness of sambrani
beyond comprehension,

thought becoming
 the deepening
of smoke lifting
 from an abalone shell

like the miracle
 of a crystallized hurt
allowing itself to breathe,

 generations not-yet-here
watching—

 their gaze
 rolling in
from the deep

## Bīja[2]

On the smooth edge
of a day almost turned
from summer's golden throb
to the burnt orange
of autumn's slow chase,
a sound spills itself out
into the day's wide pool
calling attention to itself
in the way only something
fully immeasurable can—

if it were a mirror
it would catch the light,
silently sending out
a sound that cannot be ignored
or traced, except in the way
everything keeps circling
back to it, as if the entire day
had grown from this one
intrinsic seed

---

[2]*Bīja* = seed sound

**Birdsong**

Winding staircases
  of light
in the song
  of a bird

 the vibration
of trills
  flowering
into something
  remembered
deeply

in hearts
  winged
by long lifetimes
  sky-vast

**Blessing**

Three hawks sweeping down
   from the mountaintops
glide over acres
   of graves—
the smooth curve
   of their wings
blessing the bones
   resting, free from flesh,
inside metal and wooden wombs
   inside the belly of the earth,

the souls, born into
   a new realm, soaring
beyond the hawks,
   returning, hovering,
alighting periodically
   to watch
loved ones
   placing flowers,
clearing the new growth
   covering over
the names and dates
   carved into the granite
long ago

**Bloodwork**

Today, with its caverns
of light tunneling the heart,
is a day for opal, turquoise,
copal, and sage, beauty
burning through
the ash sitting in clumps
on the tongue, words
fallen from flame,
the planets torqueing
the skies sending
spirals of thunder
traced with lightning
into the most remote
veins, the chambers
of the heart where
a *legato* woven
of unnamed intricacies
plays on, etching
its rhythm into the hollows
of the bones, the marrow,
despite it all, still singing.

**Bone Blessed**

Exquisite skeletal
  architecture,
resonance
  of earth's minerals
in bones' song:

 femur, tibia, fibula,
sacrum, vertebrae,
   shoulder blade,
  humerus, radius,
ulna, skull—

  the symmetry
of teeth and nails—

  the mineral imprint
in hair flowing
  into tresses,

the smooth arcs
  of half-moons of eyebrows,

the fluttering of eyelashes
  encircling the globes
peering out
  from the rounded nests
of orbital sockets,

  the silent harmony
of their ancient
  duet
skull-deep

**Brocade**

The texture of a voice
   embossed with gold,

the shimmerings
    of joy woven
   into each word,
each laugh,
   each pause—

Syllables glowing…

The luminosity of logic
   spun with intuition's grace
into designs
   ensorcellingly ornate
      as wisteria

**Butterfly**

At the base
of the throat,
a hidden butterfly
conducting
a symphony…

tempo
increasing
decreasing
the speed
of the pulse,
the whir
of the mind

the silent
mystery
of the
symmetry
of the winged
space
at the throat
unseen

## Cartography

Maps on the palms,
  the soles of the feet—

astronomers,
  astrologers,
 sailors
  reading the skies

like *vaidyas*[3] reading irises and tongues,
  entire worlds embedded
in a line here, a marking there,

the terrain telling a story
  like every turn in the road,
every ditch, every valley,
  every mountaintop in a range
where an ocean
  and its everlasting waves
once sung

---

[3] *vaidya*= Ayurvedic physician

**Center-Song**

Center-song
  of a mother's
memory

Center-song
  of a mandala
expanding—

Between
  Xiphoid process,
and pubic symphysis,
  navel blossoming

Center-song
  like the core
    of the earth,
the core
  of a mango,

the crux
  of an issue
remembering
  its birth,
where it came from:
  how it was sung
with great devotion,
  into being

## *Chelonioidea*[4]

Night eyes awake see something moving
impossibly out of the surf, black waves
against black sky, as if something
could transverse the two worlds of land and sea,
as if there were a language
born of both water and earth,
as if it were possible to trust
a dream giving birth to itself
on the edge of an island
nested deeply within the ocean
of time

Beached upon the shore of memory,
gasping, the years washing over in waves,
enormous turtles swimming
through the sea of night, crawling up
onto the sand like secrets

traveling later back into the ocean
that coughs up neither past or future
but remains as it is,
with only the moon as witness,
tracing the ancient curves
of the turtles' shells with light

---

[4] *Chelonioidea*: scientific name for sea turtles

**Cicada Song**

Cicada-song pulsing
   seventeen-years strong—
blooming with otherworldliness:

An ongoing meditation
   rising from the earth,
visiting as if from another planet,
   transforming the texture of the air,

the vibration wrapping around
   every leaf, every twig,
the medulla oblongata
   of every living being

**Circling**

In a circle,
  trees swaying

In a circle,
  memories
weaving together
  like vines

In the circling

  forgetting
and
  remembering
and
  forgiving

  forgetting
and
  remembering
and
  forgiving

singing
  themselves

singing
  themselves

     free

**Cocoon**

Immersion
in transformation
so deep
it appears
as darkness—

The future wings
of this
too far away
to see
or touch

For now,
just a slow
spinning,

inside
a thickening,

everything else
lost—
utter focus
on breath
defeating death

as the silken thread
of the Self
begins
to renew

**Collaboration**

Sitting in the center
of a forest,
the choir of trees
blessed with light,
creekwaters nearby
rippling…

A breeze gently
moving across
a face, eyes closed,

steady rhythm
of breath
flowing in and out

Mind, body, spirit
resonating
with the earth,
water, fire, air,
space—

spaciousness,

abundance
within

mirroring
　the illimitable
depth
　of the sky

**Colors Reconfiguring**

Embroidered in the heart center,
  a word
grown from the vibrant thread
   spooling forth
    from the center of each sound,
each experience, each moment
   recorded in the
*sanctum sanctorum*[5]
  the inner chamber
    grown
in the womb's slow weave,
   the collage of molecules
in a mandala
   blooming anew,
designs and colors reconfiguring
   with each inhalation
     of light

---

[5]*sanctum sanctorum:* holiest of holy; the innermost sacred chamber of a temple

**Cores Steady**

A year without
  daffodils,
their yellow faces
  lost to a world
gone mad—

The trees replicating
   patterns in the veins
of their leaves,

  their roots expanding
unseen,

  their cores steady
with a wisdom
  born of seeing
plagues, deaths,
  betrayals
come
  and
go
  come
  and
    go

**Could You Become**

Could you become a hawk—
    not a hawk—
        but the flying free—
    the gliding—
        the soar-over-the-mountains—
the no-longer-needing-the-ground—
    the softness—
        could you become—
a tree—
        not a tree—
        but the gentle swaying—
the not-needing-to-search—
    a safe space for hawks to rest—
the giving into seasons—
    standing strong—
           when stripped bare—
every raw place exposed

**Courage**

Encased in darkness—
  light no longer
remembered—

 only endlessness,
the howl of the shadow
 of the moon—

Relentlessly,
 some force within
moving upward—
 into what?

Tunneling up, up,
 slowly—days—
weeks—
 until bursting

 into a forgotten
abundance,

 embracing
a brilliant sky
 bedazzled
    by the sun

 drenched
in the unwavering
 loveliness
of its
  effulgence,

the immeasurable
  splendor
 of its
  radiant
        light

## Cradling Dissonance

A wooden hand cradling dissonance:
sirens wailing past swaying bamboo,
Queen Anne's Lace lining the roads
threading through the space
occupying the place where rivers
may begin to flow

It is the right time
disguised as the wrong time,
lost ships welling up
from the sacrum, thigh, hip

Someone singing in another language
melts the grapefruit spoons
that have been scooping out
the heart into a silver pool
of light, the heart now a nest,
the shoulder blades hinging into wings,

the wasps of shredded faith
bedding down in a hive
in the furthest corner of the mind
where silent hawks trace figure eights
softening the sting into the warm sweet
of ginger, wilted fears giving way
to a universe expanding
into the liberating limitlessness
of the wingspan
of night

**Crosspollinating**

Seashells
  sitting atop
a table
  in desert sun

A cactus plant
  transported
in a backseat
  across the country
to the shore
  breathing in moist air
for the first time

Sea oats, dried,
  filling a ceramic vase
in the Midwest
  remembering the warmth
of the dunes,
  the texture of ocean air
dancing them alive

A stone embroidered
  with a fossil
from a sun-baked canyon
  open to a cobalt sky
brought to the coast
  and forgotten,
seafoam
  eddying
around it
  before
washing
  back
    out
    to
sea

**Dawn**

Birds' voices shaping
the energy field of dawn,

the vibrations of their songs
blessing the day

Our molecules
absorbing the textures
of the bird songs
crisscrossing the air
in networks
of electromagnetic waves
transmuting
the thought waves
we send out
into the world,
the silent prayers
we lift up

The wings
  of our words
    taking flight

**Deciphering**

The hieroglyph
pulsates,
its meaning
locked within
another time

The fingers
that drew
the petroglyphs
dissolving
centuries ago

Even the hands
that carved
initials
into the trees
long gone

The birds
that watched
as they flew
past
gone, too—

only the sun
and moon
as witnesses
remain,
awash
in the beautiful
unseen molecules
of space
and air

**Dimensions**

Birds argue over
  sunflower seeds
Wings fluttering
  into squawks

Bird feeder
  swaying
in the wind

Unseen, ants quarrel
  over crumbs
large enough to them
  to be small planets

Realities orbiting,
  multiple tiny galaxies
merging into one

**Early Morning**

Early morning
  on the cusp
     of dawn
   the birds in India
sending their song
  through incense-sweetened
air, ghee candles flickering
  on altars,
fresh flowers
  of hibiscus and jasmine,
garlands of marigolds,
  the smell of camphor,
wildgrown herbs swaying
  in the breeze,

milk in the coconuts
  of the nearby trees
receiving the vibration
  of chanted mantras
weaving sacred sounds
   into the skies

**Earth Day**

Emerging from the rock,
  the earth, the mountaintop—
seven deer, nearly trotting—
  their brown skin
    moving across
the brown earth,
  the desert shrub—

Rarely seen here,
  nearly ten years passing
since they—
  or perhaps their parents—
last appeared

  as messengers
of an upcoming journey,
  a soul preparing
to transmute

**Earth's Aria**

From the knobby angularity
  of cacti rising six feet tall
out of the desert dirt,
  bright blooms
of fuchsia and yellow

The surrounding chorus
  of sage, piñon, and cedar
sending their blue-green hum
  into the arid sky,

their music echoing
  the song of their sisters—
the algae and seaweed
  chanting faithfully
    at the bottom
of the sun-and-moon-gilded sea

**Elixir**

Butter-yellow blooms
   against a sapphire sky

Softness of blossoms
   moving in a desert wind

Where lizards dart
   and chase,
a snapdragon kingdom
     thrives

What is the elixir
   birthing such beauty
out of sun-baked soil?

**Encircling**

Word touches center,
   takes hold

The colors, radiant,
   radiate in a pattern
rhythmed not unlike the sun
   as it traces the faces
of petals spinning softly
   from some central song

The circle widens
   chasing slowly
the fold
   where one line
spills into the next
   shapeshifting
from lotus
   to triangle
to crescent
   of the moon,

cascading lines,
   rippling themes,
and still,
   the intricacies
traveling back,
   always to center

Each voice a stitch
   in the encircling design

At the center of each voice,
   the full moon

**Excavation**

The trapdoor of the shoulder
leads to the *Well, I couldn't possibly*
part of the soul. It tunnels beneath
the city of unspokeness. A city folded
into itself like a bad dream.
The shoulder, content to hinge
arm to chest, will not mention
any of this. It will deny it
if asked. Instead, it will continue
to protect the hidden world
of the past by reaching forward
and further. Then, in the quiet,
from deep below, a wail will rise up
in a slight pulsing, a circling soreness.
The cry of a city abandoned.
Waiting. Even Pompeii, buried by lava
and centuries, saw the sun again.
The trapdoor cannot be bolted.
A vein of consciousness, a breath,
it beats in time with time.

**Facets**

From any angle, the light
   strums against the small face
of this moment,
    its surface
chiseled gently by the breath
   washing in and out

calmly moving
  back and forth
seemingly effortlessly
  like the pulse
keeping us in our skin

while all around us
   jet streams
of information
  and misinformation
cloud our skies
  with threats
of fronts moving in

The moon
  with its many faces
does not buy into this,
   the dark jewels of fear
outshone by the wild, sweet glow
   of a light that feeds upon night,
leaving bright shadows
   in its wake

**Fire Song**

Sun's fiery heat
   relentless,
scorching everything
   it touches,
melting patience away

Across the world,
   tiny flames
floating on sacred rivers

Fire ceremonies
   in sweat lodges,
temples, and caves
   blessed with chanting
illuminating the night

In distant forests
   and deserts
stories and laughter,
   faces glowing,
crackling flames
   of campfires
luminous
   and
      bright

**Forgetting**

Lilacs' soft purple scent
  no longer blooming
in the *callosum*
  of a mind
no longer irrigated
  by the songs of the sun,

Forgetting
  the way sun warms wheat
swaying in a field
  revered by cows,

Forgetting
  the way sun gleams
  on a river
reminding the earth
  of what it means to pray,

Forgetting
 the way
   the sun
cradles
   the night
chanting
  backward
    slowly
   into
dream

**Formlessness and Form: A Sestina**

Some say: do not adhere to a specific form—let it flow,
rushing and coursing, swept by the current
with its ancient rhythms sung down by the rain
and the twist and spin of windblown leaves,
the pulling in and eddying around the gray rocks,
the fading of everything into a rising mist.

And what do we know of near collisions, missed
by a glitch of this, a change of that, the flow
of cause and effect the force that rocks
us right out of our sleep, our current
moment, no more or less permanent than the leaves
growing and falling, budding again in the rain.

And which alphabets of truth reign
over the tongues that attempt to speak? Missed
connections—the one who arrives just after one leaves
and who's to say this isn't part of the flow,
the loosening of all control, the undeniable current
of breath slowly softening bitter, stubborn rocks?

Embedded in the rivers of thought, rocks
give the water a form to ripple around. The rain
dissolving into the river, disappearing into the current
mixing skywater with earthwater, sending it up in mist
at dawn—the molecules, the cycles, the flow
of all that arrives and all that leaves

tossing in the gap life leaves
when it's through. The way it rocks
any semblance of steady, challenging the flow
of even breath, the ragged voices that rein
in even the most enlightened, certainty fading to mist.
Unavoidable, the inevitability of the current

unable—unwilling?—to slow or stop, the current
drama not enough. Stuck on branches, the leaves
accept their lot, not howling because of missed
chances to live as antelope or seals sunning on rocks.
A golden day blowing open into a driving rain,
stiffening eventually into river ice—silent flow.

And if the rocks soften into mist,
other current forms may follow. The flow
of rain into open lips, the everywhere of leaves.

**Galaxy Within**

Hovering
within the sutures
of the cranial plates
half-thoughts
existing
outside of language

Abalone cranial plates,
a Pangaea
of tectonic plates,
movement
imperceptible

Territories mapping
the skull:
ethmoid, sphenoid,
frontal, parietal,
temporal, occipital

Boundary lines—
coronal suture,
sagittal suture,
lambdoidal suture,
squamosal suture—
dissolving in the shared space
of a smoothly-curved skull,
thoughts, like billions
of galaxies,
shining[6]

---

[6] galaxies within the skull: a concept learned from Dr. Vasant Lad

**Geography**

Continents slowly split apart
our mapped-and-charted world
Land drops off into murky depths
What we thought could not move, shifts—

Petroglyphs sleep, dreaming
in cave dwellings, well-hidden
Rocks crumbled from now-flat mountains
keep quiet about their former heights

Crashing waves of a long-dried sea
and the last pterodactyl's searching calls
echo in memories muted
by the slow evolution of our ears

## Geology of Breath

From the cliff of bone
to the sea of breath
to the raw pit of fire
just barely beginning to burn
inside a muscle, a thought,
the open space between

From the centrifugal imaginings
spinning out from memories
misplaced, replaced,
not quite erased
to the hidden caves of doubt
collapsing in the shaking
of the earth of the flesh

From the genetic glide
of all things past—
slim fossils imprinted
on the undersides of bones—
to the new cells blossoming
in quiet spaces unseen,
the breath in all seasons
warming the corridor
of the spine

**Gone Now**

In the desert of grief,
  the earth itself
shaking

  Trees suddenly wild
in a surge of wind
  sprung from
some unknown place

Winter's fierce
   endlessness
  lingering
   in the periphery
of the soul

  Ancestors,
even those
 from long ago,
   inexplicably
appearing,
   their presence
    as palpable
    as sunset's
vermillion hum

## Grasslands

i.
The sky so full like all that ever was
and the grasses their sway enough to slow
the hurry of all that trying to be first
Here is the opening to what you fear
the wide open of silence blizzards and drought
How much you love fences walls
doors and the keys that lock them
How little you are how little you know
about the difference between lonely and alone

ii.
The tall grasses golden ripple the way of waters
moving in waves and it is sea here with nowhere to go
but everywhere and you too could split like the earth
cracked open by the sun that has no trees to break its fall
here on the prairie where the only constant
is the movement of the wind
the only proof that there is anywhere else but here
that if you run to the edge of what you see
there will still be something more

iii.
The power lines stitch a seam across and beyond
the earth here knows how to stay out of the sky's way
and in the dusk returning there are only horses
moving in the delicate fires washing away the day
Look at the prairie church out there like a ship sunning itself at sea
No sign that there was once a blizzard so white
it was the fire from wooden pews
that kept the near-dead from dying

**Harvest**

A thought grows,
expanding in an instant
from a seed
to an enormous plant,
its leaves large enough
to serve as plates
for full-course meals

In just as quick of an instant
the leaves wilt and drop,
the thought cut off
from its source

The garden of the mind
rotating its crop
at warp speed,
its soil plowed gently
with each upturn
of the breath

## Heard and Unheard

Listen. The ancestors of birds
flocking and soaring
above the mountains
are singing their morning songs
at the vibration of light,
their music, no longer bound
by the reaches of small lungs,
widening into the silent spaces
inside trees

Listen. The smooth moo-ing
of a cow resting on the grass,

the nearly transparent creekwaters
rippling over rocks,

the snake contemplating
taking shelter in the wall
of an unsuspecting house,

the squirrels chasing
not so much each other
but the sheer exhilaration
of being alive

**Heart Song**

Soft green
  flowering
of light
  blooming
into a spiral
  like a
Fibonacci design
  slowly growing,
merging
  into a frequency
echoing
  a *rangoli*[7] design
made of stars,
  the heart
of the universe
  beating inside
the paradigm
  of the pericardium,
its song
  like a sweet nectar,
a divine fragrance
  merging
into a continuum
  of hearts,
sacred as a bird's heart,
  the center
of song

---

[7] *rangoli*=a geometric design made with flower petals or colored sand

**Heat**

Molten lava—
   the fireball of heat
at earth's core—

   blood boiling
in a fever unrelenting,
   the way sun scorches
pale skin,
   wilts the crops,

the burning of a fire ant
   caught in a paw,

liver inflamed
   with anger, brooding,

a hot wind
   chasing sparks
into wildfires
   eating a forest
alive

## Herald

In the yard, a robin—
the dull red of its belly
 a distant echo
of cardinals' bright
 red wings—

cone cells of the eyes
 delighting
in the reverberation
 of color,

long-dormant joy
 finding its way
through the tunnel
 of winter's bleakness
bursting into song

## Hope

Hope
  like delphinium
flowers,
  their blue petals
scattering

  conjuring
dolphins
  gliding
in a distant sea,

  the water sparkling
like calm words
  of an elder
saying very little
  yet saying
so much

**Impermanence**

Deep inside
the darkest core
of night,
claws digging
into the soil,

a skunk
hungry
for grubs
slicing the roots,
sending dirt
flying

In the morning,
he, and the larkspur—
gone

Tall stalks
of green
with blue
and white
blossoms,
all of it
trampled:

the slow-growing
sweetness
destroyed
swiftly
beneath
a waning
moon

### In the Silence in Between

The rabbits and deer—
   even the air—
  becoming still

The frogs, crickets,
  and birds—
their songs
  disappearing
into silence

A purple light
  blooming
inside
  carrying
the language
  of the sky

**Inside the Flow**

Unspoken,
   unwritten,
     a message
   travels
across the world
    swiftly

  the way
fear scatters birds
  from treetops,

  the way
peace
  brings a bird
to perch
  on a meditator
remaining
  deep
inside
  the flow

**In the Mind**

In the mind of a goose
looking at a lake

In the mind of a squirrel
scampering up a tree

In the mind of a gnat
being swatted at

In the mind of a cow
chewing its cud

In the mind of a cat
snoozing in the sun

In the mind of a snail
inching across the street

In the mind of a horse
galloping at dawn

In the mind of a snake
slithering beneath a rock

In the mind of a dolphin
leaping out of the sea

In the mind of a human
gazing up at the sky

In the mind, a mind
remembering its true Self

**Interwoven**

In the center of the ribs,
in small caves, old ones chant,
invoking the grace of heaven
with the geometry of their prayers,
their words, patterned like constellations,
carving out small tunnels of light

In the center of the eyes:
bright stars carrying the news
from galaxies untranslatable
except in the way the reverberation
of a church bell encompasses centuries
sharing the same central sound

In the center of the palms,
slight etchings of generations
crisscrossing in gentle pathways
not unlike the way one breath
braids briefly with another,
crosscurrents in the river of time

## Into Equilibrium

In a copper container
　encased in brick—
dried cow-dung patties
　burning with camphor,
ghee, frankincense[8]

Pungent smoke
　lifting up—
transmuting the air,
　modifying molecules,

smoothing the vibrations
　only the mosquitoes, flies,
spiders, and ants can hear

The cosmos coming
　into equilibrium
slowly—

like a hint of wind
　finding the high reaches
of the mountain—
　just enough
to make
　the prayer flags
flutter

---

[8] *agni hotra*: an ancient Vedic healing fire ceremony

## Jewels

Like clusters
of grapes
grown plump
in the sun,
the spherical jewels
of the lungs:
alveoli

Alchemy
  delivering oxygen
to red blood cells—

The very essence
  of life
transpiring,
  inspiring,

spooling out
  from such
humble
  gems
divinely
  designed
so long ago

**Koan**

Hours of years of early morning meditations
pulse on the silent globes of closed eyes
the way a lavender plant given after a death
keeps turning its leaves toward the light

Molecules of skin reconfigured
by long nights of chanting
in a music not unlike the birth of a star

The immensity of darkness, atrocities
etched in the heart giving way
in the stillness, the quiet—
the brilliance on the other side
of every sour-rotted thing
splitting open into song

**Letting Go**

i.  alpha & omega

Is it not the solace of birth
that keeps the decaying bones singing?
Birth of a forgiveness nearly tangled to death
in its umbilical cord; birth of a chance
as unlikely as lilac in a prison yard,
its sweetness arresting the wild eyes.
Birth of that which does not know
what it is except for knowing
it has never been before.  First cry,
air pushing through lungs of disbelief,
floor filled with afterbirth—
the only evidence of labor, the long gestation,
the willingness to carry, like Charon's angel,
ferrying across dark waters, the thin river
between worlds, the glistenings
of their reflections, the way the first breath
and last mirror each other, gentle
and desperate in their unknowing


ii.  preparing

Backwards, the sweep—
   decades tidying up,
     monumental decisions, now dust,
  the vacuuming out, crevices
    of mind and heart clearing,
soles of the feet
   and pelvic floor scrubbed clean,
  the laundering of remnants,
    old scraps of thought caught
on the bronchial branches, washed,
   folded, and put away,
     all the small round windows
   and mirrors of circulating cells
    wiped free of their smudges, and
in the endless kitchen of memory,

    the most delicious aroma is stirring
the flavors of the past gathering,
  soul shining like just-polished silver,
skin loosening, a worn apron whose work is done,
  the breath, a rough wind gently dying down


iii.  owl-dreamt,

a cricket-spiced wind,
the roofs of childhood leaning,
everybody waiting spoonful by spoonful,
breath by breath, pulse wild
with leaving, boats knocking
against the dock, hearts heaving,
the buoys in the bay nowhere
to be found, compass of bone
and star, sails sewn of curtains, bedspreads,
wedding dress, the lurching into,
the swimming out of, the boat
of the body lifting its wings, head swiveling,
one more time, looking back, then
up, speckled and soaring, glow
of sanctuaries and saints, swallow of light,
and then


iv.  what remains

Lymphatic tissue, once emphatic, now gone.
In the cavity where a heart pumped, just air.
Twin lobes of the lungs now the hollows of ribs.
The tongue that chose its words so carefully, absent.
Nasal passages sifting the breath no longer needed.
The webbing of skin between thumb and forefinger, long gone.
Which is not to say that all softness is lost.
Look at the gentle curve of the humerus,
how the slow scoop of the skull
mirrors the harvest moon.

**Liminal**

Right before
the flowerbud
opens

The glimmer
of a new idea

Just as a storm
is brewing,
clouds thickening

Right before
the first birdsong
at dawn

The initial
vortex
of a maelstrom

In between
dendrite
and axon

The sacred
center

between
inhale
and
exhale,

pulsing

**Listening to the Underside of Leaves**

Turtles, their slow breath.
A flute song for somebody's mother
rising to the sun. Large rocks with painted faces
watching over the empty space.
Fields where mustangs toss their manes.
A canoe gliding silently beneath the low branches.
Hands dipping pine needles into earth-paint
drawing infinity on the curved sides of dried gourds.
The monkeys swinging overhead
chattering with red birds as they pass.

**Looking Within**

The rich scaffolding of rib and spine

Exhibits in the gallery
of the heart, ever-changing

A thick tapestry of deftly woven fibers
draping the marbled wall of every bone

Like tiny stained-glass rose windows,
each carefully rounded cell, shining

The hair, rich strands of moonlight,
the nails, the finest of jewels

Embroidered on every mosaic
in the winding hallways of the mind:

golden threads born over and over
in the generous spool of the breath

**Looking: The Five Elements**

i.  Looking into the Wind

a million tongues collide
in the way atoms combine
in each word designed
by voices now mute in the slow dissolve
of matter into space, the wind not privy
to definitions of time, the recent past,
ancient empires, and pre-Columbian eras,
a flow unobstructed, dialects disregarded,
translations not needed, every syllable resurrected
and walking on its own two legs into silence, the cosmos
in which all speaking merges into one,
beyond tongue, beyond ear, beyond any revolution,
involution, evolution of what this world can carry


ii.  Looking into the Ether

there is salt, flocks of it,
white wings catching the light,
salt from the sea, salt from the brow,
salt from the mines, salt from the bread,
salt that doesn't even know where it's from,
the salty sound of voices crackling
cyberoptically profound words that are only
particles of sound, scattered, the seasoning
of what must be said into the soup of silence,
simmering as it has for ages, unbeckoned
by the newest recipes, the latest ways
to say x+y+z equals something
you must taste for yourself

iii.  Looking into the Water

there is nothing but lava
molten fire erupting
bubbling up from the core of a song
composed in aquamarine,
rhythmic waves, tranquility
of absolute transparency, the currents
synchronized with the luminous moon
not batting an eye at the seed of fire
hidden inside the song, knowing it must rise,
even with water in its lungs, spew forth,
and not, not, not be tamed to implode
but shake the clear waters
free from their lull
fill their clear vessels
with primordial heat


iv.  Looking into the Fire

there is nothing but sleet,
centuries of it, folding into
the rhythmic waves
of a sun-sung sea,
the sea and sleet separated
by millennia, which is to say
the molecules of the mollusks
have not known the cold fury
of pelting ice yet carry it,
as they carry the ancestral wings
of gulls they have never seen
even as they glide directly above,
miles from the benthic depths,
ink-dark and just as unwritten,
wordless plots hatching unscripted,
completely on cue, Act 2
gliding into Act 3, no intermission required

v.  Looking into the Earth

the transfixed bones of bliss return,
holding the gaze, as if to say:
*what are you doing looking down*
*instead of up? And: we, too, sifted the soil*
*with our hands, searching…*
The phalanges, motionless, paint
their vanished skin of a dream,
green stripes, blue designs,
a language of crushed berries and herbs,
the pelvic cradle rocking without moving
into a rhythm sustained by joy
not compressed by the passage of time,
the capillaries slipping into dreams
of themselves, the hips no longer
hips but the space through which
the earth itself still sings

**Luminous**

A spine luminous
with generations of light

Memories interlacing
with vertebral grace

Cerebrospinal fluid
flowing smoothly
over small boulders of bone

Riverbed of the back
gleaming, conjoining
the sacral arrowhead
to the tree of life

Thoughts, like leaves,
fluttering

## Lung Song

In pockets of the lungs
forgotten griefs sleep.
Curled up in the alveoli
they pulse a thick blue-grey
imperceptible except
for the catches in the breath,
the shallow diver unable
to explore the deep,
the rich leagues below
left untouched,
the pains of the past
hardening into shells
composite of silt and sand
too far from the currents
irrigating the canals
of exhale, inhale, exhale

**Mist**

It's hard not to wonder if the mist
that shifts around these mountains
each morning is not the spirits of those
who lived here long ago, appearing
and disappearing in the thin air.

The river could tell you their names
and how they fell—tomahawk, bullet,
disease, heartbreak—but knows it's not
so much their names that matter,
but the fullness of their songs,
the strength and gentleness of their hands,
if they were grateful for the very breath
in their lungs, the chance to heal,
the wild sweetness of a night sky full of stars.

**Monsoon**

A rumbling
crescendo
coming closer

Messenger
of the sky stirring,
blessing of wild rains
washing the dry air,

Sound of the downpour
cleansing the soul,

coveted moisture
softening the air

Lightning's zig-zag
cracking open the sky
flooding the clouds
with light

**Murmurations**

Starlings sweep the sky,
wash through in waves,
thousands of beaks and feathers
collaging in patterns
of pulsing shapes

and who can explain
the choreography of this mass dance,
the airborne calligraphy
scrolling delicately

disappearing and reappearing,
reinventing itself with each crescendo,
each swelling of sound and sight
as if to say: *this is it,*

this swooping and sailing,
every song
born from their tiny lungs,
and the softest
of murmurations,

*this is it,*
the breath, the song,
the miracle,
the letting go

**Night's Choir**

Washed in light, the day slipping
away. Night flickers. Lamps illuminating
the roofed spaces walled in from the dark,
light wrapping around every blade of grass,
every empty wrapper littered along the street,
every stone, every rock. Only now
with the black of night brushed across
the loud details of day
can the bugs hear themselves think,
the pulsing of the cicadas and crickets
a tapestry of sounds
the ear cannot begin to unstitch,
ancient threads spooling into
the deep reaches of time

## Ocean of Peace

Ocean of peace—come,
   even as we are shipwrecked,
even as our lives are upended,
   wash over us
with your healing waters,
    wise in the way of generations
that have witnessed every pain,
   every loss, every suffering,

still greeting the morning
   with praise,
still meeting
   the hollow of night
with heart open
   to song,

in silence
  and in sound,
the prayer of peace
  echoing,
resounding,
   like a bell,
a gong

## Of Breath and Bone

Deep within the marrow
of the moment, a stirring

One thought articulating
with the next and another,
fleshing out the scaffolding
of a self lit by filaments
of breath

The musculature
of antithesis working against
what is rising up, birthing itself
from the osteoblast of truth
uncowed by anything but
its own genesis,

no network
of opposition strong enough
to stunt the growth
of the lifeforce blooming
one inhale, exhale at a time

**Offertory**

What if your entire life
with all its bells and whistles,
its sirens and swords,
becomes, one day, a photo
unlabeled at the back
of a photo album
about to be discarded—

Does that mean
it's not worth it
to pray
or praise
with every molecule
of your being?

What if the main message
transmits not through
the sermon
but in the violin solo
or the flute and piano duet,
their musical phrases
resonating deeper
than the words—

or perhaps rests
in the silence,
the absence,
the divinity
of simplicity,
a single flower
petal,
a rock,
a ribbon
of light

**Of Silence and Rain**

Not so much desert and ocean
as the memory of the trees
who have not forgotten at all
but rest in a beautiful deep sleep

These are the trees people call to in dreams
without ever uttering a word or parting their lips,
the topography of silence and rain
mixing together in a choir of leaves
moving in wind, a music heard
as a divine poem
or entirely skimmed past

or lingered upon for a half-second
in a brief fluttering of remembering,
the catacombs of the mind half-breathing,
candles flickering on the altar of the heart

## One Syllable

Write *light*. Watch how the air quickens.
A gentle humming begins.
Somewhere, a memory of sunrise
wakes, shakes off years of dust and debris,
and shimmers, its delicate vibrations
warming the spine,
traveling vertebra by vertebra,
an extension of song
alighting in the quiet chambers
of doubt, filling the stony caverns
with candlelight
gentle as a prayer
circling its way up from generations
of sleep, cobwebs swept clean,
marrow returning to song

**Orange**

Orange leaves—
　hundreds of them—
thousands—
　erupting
　　the mountain
into a firestorm,
　molasses-sweet

Mountains
　square-dancing
into autumn
　as if they never knew
the leafless shudder
　of trees
　　silhouetted
by the swirling
　of winter snows

## Our Tongues Split

We, bilingual in yes and no,
illusion and absolution,
perception and deception,
hate and love,
storm and salve

Our tongues split screens
of fear and faith,
speaking in ciphers,
in riddles puzzling even ourselves,
in words scented with saffron
and bacon, the gears of the clocks
of our hearts turning,

measuring how close or how far
we are from translating
the etchings on our bones
sung down like generations
born of both sun and moon

## Owl

Owl keeping watch,
  waiting—
hidden in the dark
  in the upper branches—
for the precise moment
  to reveal itself

Bold knowing eyes
  that don't blink back death
arriving, wings folded,
  as if to say: Look, watch—
this life that is here now
  will soon fly—

**Pangaea**

Through the splitting ground
of what-used-to-be
fly brilliantly-shaped birds

Forehead splits
into a million songs
forking and curling
like vines

Heart splits
open into a flock
of stars, a new galaxy
unfolding

Blooming
from the gut,
a flower rooted
deep within
slowly begins
to speak

**Pattern**

Like lace,
the intricate pattern
of memory
woven, as if by hand,
into the *substantia alba*
of the mind,

the replication
of contemplation,
the resurrection
of affection,
the integration
of hesitation,
inspiration,

the tunnels
of the mind
leading to
half-remembered
labyrinths
of lifetimes
delicate
as lace

**Perching Inside the Soul**

From an ash-battered valley
up flies a bird with red wings

This bird, swooping and rising,
could kiss the face
of a volcano spewing fire
and not lose a note
of its song, its beak carrying
a trill, reverberating
like sun on silver

Wings sifting the silence,
flapping red, shout
Yes! Yes! against whatever
shadowy doubt reaches out
toward this flash of feathers bright
against an almost graying full moon

**Portal**

Somewhere in between
where the heel and ball of the foot
press the standing body
into the earth, ground, floor,
the universe breathes

An inhalation slips through
as if a mouth rested there, unseen
the way petals opening in morning light
pull into their moist lips
the cool air still shaded by stars

The body rooting into its feet
into the invisible reaches below
growing slowly into a mountain's sure face
looking straight into the sun's blaze
as deeply as into night's deep dream

The ankles, knees, hips for a brief moment
align and open.  Into these small curves,
distant oceans of silent song wash in.
The legs, two columns of prayer,
asking and thanking, balancing, begin.

**Prairie**

Grasshoppers flying up
  out of prairie grasses swaying,
open fields—treeless—
  the earth baked and split
into puzzle pieces—
  enormous tumbleweeds
gaining speed
  in a wind that won't quit

Prayer ties of red, yellow,
  white, blue, green,
    black hanging
in the branches,
  the buttes imprinted
by the hooves
  of mountain goats,

rocks remembering
  the scent
of frankincense,
  the smoke of sage,
graceful languages of old
  lifting up
in songs
  passed down
from the sun
  and the moon

**Prayer Circles**

*Raṅgoli*[9] of flowers,
   their petals—orange, pink,
red, white, purple,
   blue, yellow—
their designs encircling
   the ground
  blessing the earth

Resonance
  of the smoothness
of cellular membranes,
   cytoplasm's silent chants
echoing inside
   the internal terrain

In sweat lodges,
   circling around the fire,
prayers lifting up

Eyes smiling,
   remembering
a beauty
  of long ago—
leaves, twigs,
   and pinecones
    placed
in a circle
  on a forest floor,

Owl-eyes observing
   from high branches—
the cosmic voices
   of distant planets
  offering their circular songs

---

[9] *raṅgoli*: a geometric pattern made of flower petals or colored sand

**Quilted**

Quilted colors of the heart
   patterned like a stained-glass
circular window
  in a chapel catching the sun,
its brilliance sung alive
   by the light

Voices quilted into minds
  sewn together by threads
    of sound,
  each voice
vibrating
  singularly
 singing
    the textures
   of colors
      awake

Quilted into dreams,
   pieces of known and unknown
resting side by side,
a crazy quilt
 of consciousness
woven
  intuitively
by all-seeing hands
   unseen

**Radius**

The center of a grain of rice
opens like a song
born of fields of rice sleeping
beneath a foreign sun,
the sun sending its warmth
in rings that circle and overlap
so it's impossible to see
where each one begins, a layering
of light moving out from center
the way hope spins out
from an indefatigable core,
or the way even a small seed
of remorse can root a forgiveness,
its branches expanding, its radius
sheltering ever more ground each year

**Remembering**

Souls born of arroyos
  howl like petroglyphs
remembering a time
  when caves still held
fires surrounded by stones
  late into the night,

the stars listening from afar,
  the coral in distant seas
no longer comforted
  by saltwaters' sway,

clouds remembering
  without remembering,
the days, the years

Entire centuries
   appearing
  and
disappearing

Herbs in remote mountain
   remembering
both the touch of those
    who removed their leaves
  without first blessing
    the moon

and the touch of those
   who received their leaves
with the gratitude
  and grace
of a devotee,
   finally reaching—
after a long pilgrimage—
  the temple door

**Resilience**

Snapdragon
  plump in its greenery,
    sending soft mouths
rippling like yellow ribbons,
  golden-glowing
as if from another world,

hinting at something
  beyond
    comprehension,
beyond logic:

  the way
the snapdragon
  returns
year after year
  despite blizzard, hail,
drought—
    determined
  to send forth
its leaves and blossoms
to resurrect its dulled,
    dried husk
      into the divine
        golden miracle
      of rebirth

**Resonance**

Light streams in through tiny beams
as if millions of microscopic apertures
lined the outermost layer of the skull,
with tiny channels radiant
as sun and moon

The resonance, not knowing
or needing to know a language,
communicating effortlessly, eloquently
at the speed of light—no pause, lull,
translation, or interpretation,

the shower of light washing
the particles of indecision clean,
lasering through old paradigms
until the innermost spheres can breathe

## Rippling

In the outer banks
of memory,
rippling currents
expanding
concentrically
like the resonance,
the reverberation
of an echo—

like the vibration
of humming
spreading
from the throat
rippling out
into the cells
of the body—

like the scent
from a single
incense stick
unfurling—
spreading
its sweet calm
far and wide

**Rivers**

The mighty, humble rivers
   of the earth
like ever-flowing
  *mendhi*[10] designs
ornate with swirls
  and curves

Flowing beneath the skin,
  the vital elixirs
of plasma
  and blood,
the sacred tributaries
 of arteries, capillaries,
  and veins,

Cerebrospinal fluid
  circulating through
intricate aqueducts
 of the brain
  and cascading canals
of the spine

and when least expected,
 the sacred healing rivers
of tears
 irrigating
the tiny arroyos
 of the face

---

[10]*mendhi:* ornate designs on hands, arms, legs, feet made with henna

**Ruins**

The crow has a lot on its mind
and his voice scrapes rough
against the smooth sandstone
chipped and pressed with mud
piece by piece
into walls round as the sun
baking these rocks still

Wildgrasses shake and sway
in the place
where feet turned and stepped
in a rhythm measured evenly
like the corners of the windows
and doors that the wind wanders through
like a spirit that didn't travel on with the rest,
here to sing the slow sweet song of death
that will level our homes,
roof the ruins with sky,
and honor us with the same sun,
the same quiet
that lives within these walls

*Scherzando*[11]

High winds
  spin the limbs
of forty-year-old trees
  into a dramatic dance,
branches forgetting
  their stillness,
becoming wild
  as panthers
    uncaging
      themselves

  The storm jolting
the tall, towering beings
  into dynamic movement,
a flamenco dance
  born of years of silence,
the heart of the trees
  finally set free

---

[11] *Scherzando*: a musical cue to play in a lively manner

**Singing Bowl of the Heart**

Overhead, three gulls stitch the clouds
   with their bright blue cries

The singing bowl of the heart
   reverberating
like a slow fingertip
   sliding itself around the edges,
following the curve,

as if the ocean's calm
   has moved inside
     and our hearts are shells
not yet broken,

   mysteries
of the deep-sea floor
    embedded
in the smooth surfaces
   glistening
in the light

**Sitar's[12] Song**

Like silk, like sweet curry,
  like the fragrance of incense,
the glow of a candle, its sweet lick

  From the sitar millennia spill forth,
their molecular structures
  refracting facets unknown
spinning sounds composed outside of time,
  the large pegs turning like knobs
in the tuning aligning the spine
  of the body of music breathing in the hands
of one who savors like a delicacy
  the flavor of each note—divine

  Every atom of every note
emerging like a *maṇḍala*[13]
 from the center of surrender
player and *rāga*[14] and listeners merging
  into one

---

[12] sitar: a long-necked stringed musical instrument of India
[13] *maṇḍala*: a geometric design representing the cosmos
[14] *rāga*: a sequence of notes in Indian classical music

**Small Spaces**

In what small space
   behind the eyes
      does memory
  reside?

In what small space
   inside the cochlear curves
      does echo
  dwell?

In what small space
   beneath the root
      of the tongue
    does swallowed hurt
  sour?

In what small space
    within a fingerprint's whorl
       does the touch
    of love
  linger?

In what small space
   inside the twin caves
      of the nose,
    does the aroma of roses
  bloom?

**Smoldering**

Suddenly,
  a hot spot
flaring up
  in the lobes
of the liver—
  a spark of envy
quickly raging
  out of control

 Ego fueling
the fire

Inflamed hurt
  bursting into flame—
vitriol spewing
  from anger's fire

Heat spreading
  with each new breath,
each new word

Extinguishing slowly
  in forgiveness's
slow cooling,
  dousing,
dampening down

  Eventually,
despite stubborn
  embers,
    letting go—

## Sometimes It Is the Not Saying

Sometimes it is the gap—
the chasm—
the wide-open space
aching—
syllables, words,
and acknowledgment
all absent,
as if a meteor had not landed,
as if a hurricane had not flooded the dry land,
as if two souls coming together had never met,
as if the shattered glass had not once been whole

Sometimes it is the not saying—
words unbirthed still stuck in the mouth,
the silences yawning
like sleepless nights untold,

the echo of emptiness ricocheting
against the slow edges—blank,
vibrational frequencies gone,
syllabic cadences extinct,
transmitting signals disappeared
into the vast openness
of communication unreceived

except in the way an intuition
keeps knocking ever-so-gently
at the center of the third eye

**Song of the Potomac**

Sun shimmering
   on the Potomac,
early morning.

At Riverbend, tall trees, quiet trails,
   tranquil waters, leaves spring green.

A heron's grace. The sound
    of Canadian geese.

   A spider web's gossamer
catching a ray of light.

   In the distance
the quiet roar of waterfalls.

The woods whispering stories of long ago
   when eyes, long-ago-turned-to-dust,
gazed out at the same waters—

   and hands,
now dried and hollowed,
   gathered herbs for healing salves.

The scent of campfires
   from generations long ago
hovering in distant corridors of time.

Kayaks plying the riverwaters
   like the canoes of long ago.

   White dogwoods
singing of spring,
    their blossoms like lace.
Bright-pink dogwoods
   bursting forth with joy

Cherry blossoms'
   pastel-pink serenade
     ushering in bluebells
  by the thousands

**Temple Inside**

Inside the temple
of the heart,
flecks of gold
catching the light

Vibrations of harps,
flutes, and bells,
a cosmic chamber music
celestial, echoing
the stars

The light
of a thousand
votive candles,
illuminating,
emanating
from deep within

the spaciousness
of the sweet silence
like an enormous
cathedral
at dusk,
each one
of its pews
emptied out

## The Current, the River, and the Rain

The riverwaters gleam
a glistening black, the recent rainwaters
quivering the current. It is night
and there is nowhere to go
but everywhere. The spilling of one thread
into the next
    And this flow
does not stop does not stop does not stop.
It opens into the wingspan of morning
coasting in over the night's sprawl,
over the first sleep, second sleep,
last sleep
    The river of breath
spilling over the crests and banks
of the bones, slipping in and out
of the corridors of the lungs,
sending its currents rippling into the farthest reaches
of toe tips and palms,
      the curl and curve
of all that gives and all that gives way,
the edges letting go into something softer,
sweeter, the mirage of goodbye breaking
apart,
    the weight of a construction crane
reduced to a bright yellow leaf floating
on the Gihon River which is Powell River
and the Potomac and the Rio Grande and every river
brushing the earth with smooth, sure strokes
shaping the tides of live and the tides of die
that speak each time we breathe

**Through a Deepening Mist**

Through a deepening mist,
   mystical happenings flock in
as though migrating
   from some deep
untranslatable source,

the soul hearing
   remote colors,
touching unknown tastes,
   sounds strung
like garlands of light
   appearing
like stars embedded
   in the tongue,

like cranial constellations
   shining through the skull,
a sparkling song
   playing along the corners
of the eyes,
   not a single word
being said

**Transformation: A Sestina**

When the storms of life roar, how easily we forget the light.
Sunrise's nectar stunning us, reinvigorating us with its sweet peace.
Buried in the past, deaf to the miracles of tomorrow,
we mistake now for forever and nearly bypass hope's door.
Discreetly, bluebirds high in the branches quietly pray.
Unseen, the Great Transformation of *tamas*[15] to *sattva*[16] begins to begin…

But with so much heaviness and cloudiness, how to begin?
Mystically, a glimmer inside of sacred light
glows inexplicably, intermittently, as ancestors pray.
Tiny lizards, butterflies, hummingbirds appear—messengers of peace.
Rust on hinges for decades softens into a slowly-opening door
in a heart distantly remembering the flavor of tomorrow.

Cords of the past and ribbons of the present braid with tomorrow.
In the ongoing continuum of integration, is there a moment when things begin?
Within the flow of awareness, each breath—a door…
a door expanding, blessing us equally with shadow and light.
A melody floating in, a pathway of divine peace.
In the cosmos of eternity, the stars and clouds perpetually pray.

A precocious ant asks, "What does it mean to pray?"
Thousands of questions lifting up as today gives birth to tomorrow.
A capricious pocket of faith welcoming an ancient peace
slipping through like a breeze. Angelic choruses begin
to sing arias of love flowing from a wellspring of light
opening the soul like a portal, a mystical door.

Each moment's truth renewing us in the ever-evolving door
of now. The sky, the sea, the land, the sun, and moon pray
without praying with the radiance of devotion's light.
Sunrise becoming sunset, today letting go into tomorrow,
each day shedding its skin preparing to begin
anew, vacillating between conflict and peace.

---

[15] *tamas*: heaviness, darkness
[16] *sattva*: light, purity

In life's dance, contemplations and meditations on peace
returning us home, our Self knocking softly on the soul's door.
Do we answer, or turn away? Seasons cycle and begin
a tapestry of yes and no, stop and flow, collectively we pray
and travel into the unknowns of tomorrow
with the grace of dawn's gentle and courageous light.

Doors melt away as we bow our heads to pray.
Transformations begin in the luminous promise of tomorrow.
In the sacred opening of palms, a gentle flowering of peace and light.

**Transliterating the Silence**

Twenty years of sugarcane and melon,
a language of shadow trimmed with sun

Planets hovering, a thin stream
of remembered stars between

Meteor of wildflowers appearing
slowly, reluctant and unstoppable

the green of a richly-rained summer
growing, dwarfing the rocks, the sharp angles
folding into distant memories of themselves

crop circles and the rose windows
of cathedrals in France

the circling of water in white ceramic bowls
blessed with chants before dawn

syllables lifting like birds, one after another,
transmuting the not-yet-spoken air into song

**Tree of Tranquility**

Sheltered by sky—miles of it—
  and surrounded by prairie,
     no houses, cars, or people in sight

just the sea of wind rippling,
   the dance of branches,
     the fluttering of leaves,
       hundred-year-old roots
         reaching deep into the earth

the trunk of the tree
  expanding nearly imperceptibly
    year by passing year—

a flash of red feathers:
  a bird flying
    from one branch
      to another
        like a sudden thought
     leaping
  across a synapse

then, once again,
  the stillness
returning
  rooting
into every molecule
  a deep quiet
born of slow centuries,
  the spaciousness
of treeless miles
    all around

## Unencumbered

Thoughts covering
  the moment
like a vine—

ivy's slow crawl
  over a wooden fence—

kudzu's quick spread
  over a mountain's face,
its green leaves
  like a shout rising
over everything else—

Somewhere,
  boulders sunlit,
mesas star-sung,

  the earth unencumbered
by anything,

  embraced by space,
washed clean
  by the quiet incandescence
of dawn

## Universal

I am the river and the tree,
   rock and earth.
I am the wind and the sun,
   moon and stars.
I am the wildflowers
   and the bird calls,
the scent of boxwoods,
   and the rippling of streams.
I am sunlight on water
   in early morning quiet.
I am the darkest part of night.

I am scapula and sacrum,
   humerus and hand.
I am nose and knees,
   toes and throat.
I am skin and spine,
   fingers and face.
I am voice and breath,
   song and sleep.
I am teeth and tongue,
   heart and lungs.
I am liver and spleen,
   thyroid and brain,
arteries and joints,
   muscles and nerves.

I am earth, water, fire,
   earth, and space
I am past and future,
   yes and no
I am stillness and motion,
   silence and sound.

I am all of these
   and none of these.

I am not the body.
I am not the mind.

I, like you,
 am passing through

**Unseen**

Inexplicable
  healing light—
filtering in
  as if through a curtain
unseen

Mitochondria
  meditating
deep within
  our cells—

entire worlds
  pulsing
beneath
  our skin
like the glow
  of bioluminescence
at the bottom
  of
the sea

**Unspoken**

Silence, like dappled light,
   luminous
in its simplicity

   The way a leaf shimmers
in sunlight,

   the knitting together
of shadow
   and moonlight,

   a dialogue
unspoken,
     ancient as the stars

**Untouched by Sour Sirens**

The contours of the hills
untouched by the sour sirens
of the city are soft without knowing
they are soft.  Just as the sky
is blue without trying to, the way
the blue paint a brush is dipping into
is going to awaken a clay vase
into a cosmos so brilliant
that someone, eyes nearly glazed
after visiting so many artists' booths,
will stop—hundreds of people
orbiting—feeling
the blue piece of turquoise
that's been lodged
in their heart
for years
   release

**Vanishing Point**

In the mind of an elephant
bathing in a river in India,
the remnant of the joy of his trumpeting at dawn
lingers dahlia purple, not unlike the palladian blue
resounding from an angel's trumpet

In the rainwashed spinney nearby,
echoes of arguments distill like flowering cacti,
sharp edges becoming somehow sweet
like the firewheel at the heart of a star

**Vestiges**

Sun shining in
  through
blue curtains—

  Long ago
reawakened
  like an old film
brought to life—

  Faces from forgotten
generations
  with bright eyes,
their voices, laughter
  captured like a note
in a bottle
  tossed out, carefree,
    to sea,

into a tide
  that keeps turning,
returning—
  turning,
returning…

  before
eventually
  setting us
free

**Voice**

Like a locket
  worn daily
on the throat,
  the pulsation
of unsaid words
  in a cluster
of stars,
  clouds,
porcupine quills—

A blue flower
  of sound
about to bloom
  into gales of wind,
tongues of flame,
  the earth itself
dissolving
  into quicksand
before expanding
  into the
spaciousness
  of blue pools
  sunlit with song

**Wild Mint**

Wild mint growing
  in a patch of fertile soil
its fragrance enlivening
  the air

Further down,
  rosemary, oregano, basil
lending their rich aromas
  to the symphony
filling the air
  with vibrant songs,
flavoring the moment
  with possibility,
mouth watering
  with the sweet
bright green taste
  of joy

**Winter Solstice**

A red fox bolts across two lanes of traffic.
Snow, falling gently.

In the woods, a calligraphy of vines.
Choir of leafless trees.

A flash of color. Two cardinals.
Their red feathers bright against the gray.

Overhead a hawk sails the sky.
Four deer, just as silent, appearing.

Before sunrise, the travelling song of geese.
Dogs' barks waking the day.

Along the river half-dressed in snow and ice,
a blue heron stepping forward, lifting up.

## When All Else Fails

i.
When all else fails, drink water.
Feel the cool pour of the liquid
travel the open space of your throat.
Keep drinking. Imprints of pearls
and abalone pulse in your swallow.
The deep well of renew
is within you now.
Reach into what is there:
the power to grow gold blooms
from the dull shell of seed.

ii.
When all else fails, count your toes.
Notice the smooth arc of their symmetry,
the clear faces they lift up to the world.
They are small flocks leading you forward,
as committed to their role as the sun.

iii.
When all else fails, peel an orange.
All that bright color falling away.
The brief song of orange globes, enough.
Now, the slice of your nail carves
the no-longer-needed from the needed.
The peel no less beautiful for being thrown away.

iv.
When all else fails, clean the stove.
Scrubbing away particles of dried food
clears the chance for smooth shine.
Memories of previous meals will feed you
as you notice tiny specks lingering
like the one comment, more delicious than the food.

v.
When all else fails, fold paper.
Feel the sharp crease, watch how ends meet.
Shapes emerge! Look at the bird
born from your patient folds.

## The Journey of This Book

Three main inspirations gave birth to this book:

- ❖ *Inspiration from a mentor.* When Dr. Tom O. Phillips introduced me as a moderator and poet in the poetry segment of the online WordsAwake! Writing Conference in 2021, he mentioned that his favorite poems of mine are the ones that explore the inner terrain. This caught my attention, and I decided to look back at my poems through this lens. The result of what I found is this book; some of the poems date back twenty years while others are more recent.

- ❖ *Lifelong love and respect for nature.* I've always found inspiration, peace, and joy being in nature, whether in the woods, by the ocean, in the desert, on the plains, or simply breathing fresh air, enjoying the warmth of the sun and the glow of the moon, feeling the ground beneath me, hearing the birds, watching leaves moving in the breeze, looking at sunlight on water, and so much more. Nature is a most profound poem!

- ❖ *Āyurveda.* *Āyurveda* is a vast and beautiful science of holistic healing. It has blessed my life in more ways than I can count. One of the central concepts of *Āyurveda* is the idea that we are composed of the five great elements of earth, water, fire, air, and space. For decades, my poems have explored nature and the internal landscape of mind, body, and spirit. *Āyurveda* gave me a framework for understanding the concepts I had been writing about intuitively, as well as inspiration to explore further, and I am most grateful.

# Gratitude

I express my heartfelt appreciation to Finishing Line Press for blessing this collection with affirmation by selecting it for publication and offering kind support during the publication process.

I'm very grateful to each of my writing and poetry teachers, professors, and mentors from K-12 on up, with special thanks to Linda Ferrara, Pearl Duckett, Alan Lengel, Lynda Forsythe, Proal Heartwell, Bernis von zur Muehlen, Kate Daniels, Irena Klepfisz, Tony Mares, Gene Frumkin, Hilda Raz, Howard Cummins, Mary DeShazer, Anne Boyle, and Edwin G. Wilson.

Thank you also to the many poets who have inspired me through the years, especially Joy Harjo whose chapbook poems that I read back in the mid-90s touched me deeply and helped lead me to New Mexico where I would later encounter *Āyurveda*, the wisdom of Dr. Vasant Lad, and the five great elements of *Āyurveda*—earth, water, fire, air, and space.

Much gratitude to Dr. Tom O. Phillips for inspiring the creation of this book through his comments at the online 2021 Words Awake! Wake Forest University writing conference. Thank you, Dr. Phillips, for being such a wise and kind mentor through the years. Your guidance and encouragement have helped me tremendously.

Thank you to The Ayurvedic Institute's decades of amazing teachers, students, clients, and colleagues.

Thank you to Dr. Vasant Lad for bringing the light of *Āyurveda* to my life!

Thank you to my parents, Karen and Jim Dunlop, for their love and support.

And thank you, readers, for your divine presence!

**Julie Dunlop** is a poet, an author, and a teacher of writing, wellbeing, yoga, and Ayurveda. Her writing bridges ancient and modern; East and West; contemplation and imagination, offering an oasis for readers in which to rest, meditate, and explore. Weaving together the worlds of healing and art, Dunlop's books—*Ocean of Yoga, Honoring the Light in You,* and *Thousands of Years of Prayers*—invite deep awareness and compassion. She holds a B.A. and an M.A. in English, certification as a yoga teacher (RYT-500) through Yoga Alliance, and certification as an Ayurvedic Practitioner through the National Ayurvedic Medical Association. Celebrating the mystery and sacredness of life, Dunlop's work is heart-centered, offering a unique pathway to mind-body-spirit wellbeing.

www.ingramcontent.com/pod-product-compliance
Lightning Source LLC
Chambersburg PA
CBHW031225170426
43191CB00031B/523